INDIGENOUS MEXICAN ART
CINCO DE MAYO
COLORING PAGES FOR ADULTS

SILVER SOLVERS

Copyright:

©Silver Solvers
Printed by: Amazon KDP

Disclaimer:

This coloring book is provided for recreational and entertainment purposes. While measures have been taken to ensure the accuracy and quality of the images, the publisher assumes no responsibility for any errors, omissions, or inaccuracies that may be found in them. The images are intended to be colored by users, and the final result may vary depending on individual skills and preferences. The publisher will not be liable for any damage, loss, or inconvenience arising from the use of this coloring book. Users are advised to use appropriate coloring materials. Additionally, users are encouraged to take regular breaks and avoid visual fatigue during extended coloring sessions. By using this book, users agree to these terms and conditions.

This coloring book belongs to:

_____

www.ingramcontent.com/pod-product-compliance
Lightning Source LLC
Chambersburg PA
CBHW062111220526
45471CB00010B/3695